WHAT IS THE BOOK OF LEVITICUS?

Kids' Guides to God's Word Series

What Is the Book of Genesis?
What Is the Book of Exodus?
What Is the Book of Leviticus?
What Is the Book of Numbers?
What Is the Book of Deuteronomy?
What Is the Book of Joshua?
What Is the Book of Judges?
What Is the Book of Ruth?
What Is the Book of 1 Samuel?
What Is the Book of 2 Samuel?
What Is the Book of 1 Kings?
What Is the Book of 2 Kings?
What Are the Books of 1–2 Chronicles?
What Are the Books of Ezra & Nehemiah?
What Is the Book of Esther?
What Is the Book of Job?
What Is the Book of Psalms?
What Is the Book of Proverbs?
What Is the Book of Ecclesiastes?
What Are the Books of Song of Songs &
Lamentations?
What Is the Book of Isaiah?
What Is the Book of Jeremiah?
What Is the Book of Ezekiel?
What Is the Book of Daniel?
What Are the Books of Hosea–Micah?
What Are the Books of Nahum–Malachi?

What Is the Gospel of Matthew?
What Is the Gospel of Mark?
What Is the Gospel of Luke?
What Is the Gospel of John?
What Is the Book of Acts?
What Is the Book of Romans?
What Is the Book of 1 Corinthians?
What Is the Book of 2 Corinthians?
What Is the Book of Galatians?
What Is the Book of Ephesians?
What Is the Book of Philippians?
What Are the Books of Colossians
& Philemon?
What Are the Books of 1–2 Thessalonians?
What Are the Books of 1–2 Timothy & Titus?
What Is the Book of Hebrews?
What Is the Book of James?
What Are the Books of 1–2 Peter & Jude?
What Are the Books of 1-3 John?
What Is the Book of Revelation?

What Is the Book of
LEVITICUS?

Michael Whitworth

ISBN 978-1-971767-12-3

Published by Start2Finish
Bend, Oregon 97702
start2finish.org

Printed in the United States of America

30 29 28 27 26   1 2 3 4 5

CONTENTS

INTRODUCTION

Let's be honest: you probably didn't pick up this book because you were dying to read about Leviticus.

Nobody's favorite Bible book is Leviticus. Nobody finishes Genesis and Exodus, turns the page, and thinks, *Oh good— now we get to the part about skin diseases and burnt offerings!* If the Bible were a streaming series, Leviticus would be the episode most people skip. It's the one with no action scenes, no dramatic rescues, no seas parting or walls falling down. Just rules. Lots and lots of rules. Rules about animals. Rules about blood. Rules about mold on the walls of your house. Rules about what you can eat, what you can wear, and what to do if you accidentally touch a dead lizard.

It sounds boring. It sounds irrelevant. It sounds like the last book in the Bible that a teenager (or anyone else) would want to read.

So why should you?

Because here's the secret nobody tells you: Leviticus isn't a random collection of ancient rules. It's the answer to the most important question in the entire Bible.

THE QUESTION

To understand that question, you need to remember where we are in the story. In Genesis, God created a perfect world and placed human beings in the middle of it. They were meant to live in his presence—walking with him, talking with him, enjoying the kind of closeness that most people can barely imagine. But sin wrecked everything. Adam and Eve chose their own way over God's way, and the result was separation. They were driven out of the garden, away from the tree of life, away from God's unguarded presence.

The rest of Genesis is the story of God beginning to fix what went wrong. He chose Abraham and promised to build a nation through him—a people who would belong to God and through whom God would eventually bless the whole world. That family grew into the nation of Israel, and by the end of Genesis they were living in Egypt.

In Exodus, things got worse before they got better. Israel spent four hundred years in slavery. God raised up Moses, sent ten devastating plagues against Egypt, and led his people out through the Red Sea. He brought them to Mount Sinai, gave them his law, and then did something absolutely extraordinary: he told them to build him a house. A tent, actually—the tabernacle—where his presence would physically dwell right in the middle of their camp.

And that's where the question hits.

God is holy. Perfectly, blindingly, dangerously holy. His holiness isn't just a nice quality, like being kind or patient. It's the white-hot core of who he is. When it came in contact with sin in the Bible, people died. When Moses asked to see God's glory, God told him that no one could see his face and live.

And now this God—this holy, untouchable, overwhelming God—has moved into the neighborhood. His tent is sitting right in the center of the Israelite camp, surrounded on every side by people who lie, cheat, get angry, break promises, and fail in a thousand ways every day.

So the question is this: **How can a holy God live among an unholy people without destroying them?**

That's what Leviticus answers. Every sacrifice, every law, every ritual, every festival—all of it exists to solve that one problem. How do sinful people approach a holy God? How do they stay in his presence without being consumed? How do they live as his people in a world that pulls them in every other direction?

Leviticus is God's instruction manual for living with him.

WHAT YOU'RE ABOUT TO READ

The book divides into several major sections, and each one tackles a different part of the problem.

Chapters 1–7 deal with the sacrificial system—five different types of offerings that covered everything from worship and thanksgiving to sin and guilt. These weren't meaningless rituals. Each one taught Israel something about God's holiness, the seriousness of sin, and the cost of forgiveness.

Chapters 8–10 tell the story of the priests—the men who served as go-betweens for God and the people. You'll read about their ordination, their first day on the job, and one of the most shocking incidents in the Bible, when two of Aaron's sons were killed for approaching God the wrong way. It's a hard story, but it sets the tone for everything else: God's holiness is not negotiable.

Chapters 11–15 cover the purity laws—the rules about clean and unclean food, skin diseases, bodily discharges, and contamination. These chapters are the ones most people find strange. But they were making a point Israel needed to hear every single day: holiness touches everything. There is no corner of your life—not even what you eat for breakfast—that doesn't belong to God.

Chapter 16 describes the Day of Atonement, the most important day of the year. Once a year, the high priest entered the Most Holy Place—the inner room of the tabernacle where God's presence dwelled—and performed a ceremony that cleansed the entire nation of its sin. This chapter is the heart of the book, and it points forward to Jesus more directly than almost anything else in the Old Testament.

Chapter 17 establishes why blood matters so much. It contains one of the most quoted verses in Leviticus: "The life of a creature is in the blood, and I have given it to you to make atonement for yourselves on the altar." Every sacrifice in the book rests on this truth.

Chapters 18–20 shift from worship to everyday life. This is where God says, "Be holy because I, the Lord your God, am holy"—and then shows what holiness looks like in relationships, business, justice, and love. Right here, buried in the book most people skip, you'll find the verse Jesus called the second greatest commandment in the entire Bible: "Love your neighbor as yourself."

Chapters 21–24 cover the standards for priests and sacrificial animals, the sacred calendar of festivals that structured Israel's entire year, and a few final laws. The festivals alone are worth the price of admission—every single one of them points to something Jesus fulfilled.

Chapters 25–27 close the book with the Sabbath Year, the Year of Jubilee, and the blessings and curses of the covenant. The Jubilee—a once-in-a-lifetime reset where debts were canceled, slaves were freed, and land was returned—is one of the most radical ideas in the history of the world. And when Jesus stood up in his hometown synagogue and announced what he'd come to do, the passage he read was about the Jubilee.

WHY THIS MATTERS FOR YOU

Leviticus matters because it answers questions you didn't even know you were asking.

How serious is sin? Leviticus will show you. It costs blood. It costs life. It's not something God shrugs off.

How much does God want to be with his people? Leviticus will show you that too. The entire book exists because God refused to stay distant. He moved in. He made a way. He built a system—complicated and costly as it was—so that sinful people could live in his presence and survive.

And here's the thing that ties it all together: every single part of Leviticus points to Jesus. The sacrifices point to his death. The priests point to his role as the one who stands between us and God. The Day of Atonement points to his cross. The purity laws point to his power to make the unclean clean. The festivals point to his life, death, resurrection, and return. The Jubilee points to the freedom he came to bring.

Leviticus isn't the dusty, irrelevant rulebook people think it is. It's the blueprint for everything Jesus came to do.

BEFORE YOU START

One more thing. As you read through this book, you're going to encounter some unfamiliar territory. Animal sacrifices. Blood rituals. Rules about things you've never thought about. Some of it will seem strange. Some of it will seem harsh. That's okay. Every chapter will explain what's happening and why it matters—not just for ancient Israel, but for you.

The God who speaks in Leviticus is the same God who sent his Son. The holiness that burns through every page is the same holiness that drove Jesus to the cross. And the grace that built the entire sacrificial system—the grace that said, "I will make a way for you to come to me"—is the same grace that meets you today.

So give Leviticus a chance. You might be surprised by what you find.

Turn the page.

1

COMING TO GOD ON GOD'S TERMS

Imagine you've won a contest, and the prize is a private tour of the White House—not the regular tourist kind, but the real thing. You're going to walk through the Oval Office, sit in the Situation Room, and eat lunch in the dining room where the president eats.

Exciting, right? But here's what happens before you get anywhere near the building. You go through a background check. You pass through security screenings. You're told exactly where you can walk and where you can't. There's a dress code. There's an escort. There are rules about what you can touch, what doors you can open, and how to address people.

You might think, *It's just a building. Why all the fuss?* But it's not just a building. It's where the most powerful person in the country lives and works. The protocols aren't there to keep you out—you were invited, after all. They exist because of *who lives there*. The greater the person, the more carefully you approach.

Now multiply that by infinity. Because at the beginning of Leviticus, the Israelites weren't visiting a president. They were living next door to the Creator of the universe.

Think about where we left off at the end of Exodus. The tabernacle had just been built—God's tent, right in the middle of the Israelite camp. And then the glory of the Lord came down and filled it. The cloud descended. The fire blazed. The Creator of the universe moved in next door.

This was supposed to be good news. And it was. God wanted to live with his people. He had rescued them from slavery in Egypt, brought them through the Red Sea, given them his law at Mount Sinai, and now he was making his home among them. That's grace. That's love.

But it also created an enormous problem.

God is holy. Perfectly, blazingly, dangerously holy. At Mount Sinai, the people weren't even allowed to touch the base of the mountain while God was on it—or they would die. When his glory filled the tabernacle, even Moses couldn't go inside. The same God who loved these people enough to rescue them was so pure that getting close to him without preparation would be like grabbing a live power line with your bare hands.

So here was the dilemma. God wanted to be near his people. His people needed to be near God. But sin stood between them like a wall, and God's holiness was not something that could just be ignored. How could sinful, flawed, failing human beings approach a perfectly holy God—and survive?

That's what Leviticus answers. And it starts with the sacrifices.

Leviticus opens with God speaking to Moses from inside the tabernacle—the same tent Moses couldn't enter at the end of Exodus. The very first word is a call. God called to Moses. He wasn't hiding. He wasn't pushing people away. He was inviting them in. But the invitation came with instructions, because getting close to this God required doing things his way.

The first seven chapters of Leviticus describe five different types of offerings. Each one served a different purpose, and together they formed a complete system for how people could worship God, deal with their sin, express their gratitude, and maintain their relationship with him.

If that sounds complicated, don't worry. We'll walk through each one. And as we do, watch for something important: every single offering teaches us something about what it costs to be in a relationship with a holy God—and how far God was willing to go to make that relationship possible.

THE BURNT OFFERING

The burnt offering was the most basic and most dramatic of all the sacrifices. Here's how it worked.

A worshiper would bring an animal—a bull, a sheep, a goat, or if they were poor, a dove or pigeon. The animal had to be the best they had. No injured animals. No sick ones. No leftovers. It had to be without defect—perfect.

The worshiper would bring the animal to the entrance of the tabernacle. Then they would place their hand on the animal's head. This wasn't a pat on the head. It was an act of identification. The worshiper was saying, in effect, "This animal represents me. What happens to it happens on my behalf."

Then the animal was killed. Its blood was splashed against the sides of the altar. And the entire animal—every piece of it—was burned up on the altar. Nothing was saved. Nothing was eaten. It all went up in smoke.

The text says the smoke rose as "an aroma pleasing to the Lord." That doesn't mean God was literally sniffing the air. It means he accepted the offering. It meant the worshiper's devotion had reached him.

The burnt offering was about total surrender. The whole animal was consumed because the whole point was giving everything to God—holding nothing back. It was a way of saying, "I belong to you. All of me."

And notice this: the offering "made atonement" for the worshiper. That word—atonement—is one of the most important words in the entire Bible. It means to cover over, to make things right between you and God. The animal died so the worshiper didn't have to. Something innocent paid the price for someone guilty.

THE GRAIN OFFERING

Not every offering involved an animal. The grain offering was made from the best flour, mixed with olive oil and frankincense. Sometimes it was baked into cakes or wafers. No yeast was allowed, and no honey—but every grain offering had to include salt.

Why salt? Because salt was a sign of a lasting covenant. In the ancient world, sharing a meal with salt meant you were bound together. Adding salt to the offering was a reminder that this wasn't a one-time transaction. It was part of an ongoing relationship between God and his people.

The grain offering represented the fruit of someone's labor. Flour didn't just appear—someone planted the grain, watered it, harvested it, and ground it. Bringing it to God was a way of saying, "Everything I have comes from you, and I give it back with gratitude."

A portion was burned on the altar. The rest went to the priests. This was practical as well as spiritual—the priests didn't own land or grow crops, so offerings like this were how they ate.

THE PEACE OFFERING

If the burnt offering was about surrender and the grain offering was about gratitude, the peace offering was about fellowship. And it's the most unusual of the five, because it ended with a meal.

The worshiper brought an animal—a bull, a sheep, or a goat—and followed a process similar to the burnt offering: hand on the head, the animal killed, blood splashed on the altar. But unlike the burnt offering, the whole animal wasn't burned. Only the fat and certain internal organs were burned on the altar. The rest was divided up. The priests got the breast and the right leg. And the worshiper got to eat the rest.

Think about that. A person brought an offering to God, and then sat down and ate a meal in his presence. The peace offering was a celebration. It was like being invited to dinner at God's house.

There were different reasons people brought peace offerings. Sometimes it was a thanksgiving meal—something good had happened and they wanted to celebrate. Sometimes it was connected to a vow they had made. Sometimes it was simply spontaneous—they just wanted to be near God.

One rule stood out: the meat had to be eaten quickly. A thanksgiving offering had to be finished that same day. Other peace offerings could carry over to the next day, but not beyond that. Nothing was to be kept until it started going bad. This rule probably encouraged generosity too—if you couldn't eat it all yourself, you had to share it with others.

THE PURIFICATION OFFERING

Now things get more serious. The purification offering—sometimes called the sin offering—dealt with the contamination that sin created.

This is a concept we don't always think about. We understand that sin is wrong—that it breaks God's rules. But in Leviticus, sin is more than a broken rule. It's a kind of pollution. It contaminates the sinner, it contaminates the community, and—here's the shocking part—it even contaminates the tabernacle, the place where God lives. Every sin Israel committed was like throwing mud on the walls of God's house.

The purification offering was designed to clean up that mess. The ritual varied depending on who had sinned. If the high priest sinned, the consequences were most severe, because his sin affected the whole community. If a regular person sinned, the offering was smaller but still required. Even unintentional sins needed to be dealt with.

The blood of the purification offering played a special role. Instead of just being splashed against the altar, it was sometimes sprinkled in the tabernacle itself, applied to specific pieces of furniture. The blood was literally cleaning God's house—purifying the sacred space so that God's holiness and Israel's sinfulness could coexist without God having to leave.

That's the real fear behind the purification offering. If sin built up long enough and wasn't dealt with, God's presence would eventually depart. He wouldn't live in a polluted house. The purification offering kept the tabernacle clean and kept God close.

THE GUILT OFFERING

The guilt offering—sometimes called the reparation offering—was the most specific of the five. It applied when someone had cheated another person, stolen something, lied under oath, or violated something sacred that belonged to God.

What made the guilt offering different was that it required restitution. It wasn't enough to bring an animal and ask for forgiveness. You also had to make things right with the person you had wronged. If you stole something, you returned it—plus twenty percent. If you cheated someone, you repaid them—plus twenty percent.

God wasn't interested in people who said "sorry" but didn't change anything. The guilt offering taught a critical lesson: forgiveness and responsibility go together. You don't get right with God while leaving a trail of damaged people behind you. You make it right with them too.

THE PRIESTS' INSTRUCTIONS

The first five chapters of Leviticus describe the offerings mainly from the worshiper's perspective—what to bring, why, and how. Chapters 6–7 go back over the same offerings but from the priests' point of view. They cover the practical details: how to tend the altar fire (which was never allowed to go out), which portions of the offerings belonged to the priests, how to handle the ashes, and what to do with the leftovers.

One detail stands out. The fire on the altar of burnt offering had to burn continuously—day and night, without exception. Imagine being an Israelite camped in the wilderness. You step out of your tent in the middle of a pitch-dark night, and you look toward the center of the camp. There, rising above the tabernacle, you see the glow of the fire and the smoke climbing into the sky. The fire never went out. God's altar was always lit. His presence was always there.

That fire was a constant reminder: the King is in residence. He's awake. He's watching. He hasn't left.

WHAT THIS MEANS FOR US

First, sin is serious. The sacrificial system wasn't a simple, painless process. Animals died. Blood was spilled. The message was unmistakable: sin costs something. It always has. We live in a world that likes to minimize sin, to wave it away with an "everybody makes mistakes." Leviticus says otherwise. Sin is so serious that something has to die to deal with it.

Second, God provided the solution. The Israelites didn't invent the sacrificial system on their own. God gave it to them. He was the one who said, "Here's how you deal with your sin. Here's how you approach me. I'll make a way." The God who demanded holiness was the same God who made holiness possible. That's grace.

Third, the offerings point to Jesus. Every sacrifice in Leviticus casts a shadow toward the cross. The burnt offering—total surrender? Jesus gave himself completely. The grain offering—the best of someone's life and labor? Jesus gave his entire life. The peace offering—a meal that restored fellowship with God? Jesus said, "This is my body, given for you" (Luke 22:19). The purification offering—blood that cleanses sin? The New Testament says Jesus' blood "purifies us from all sin" (1 John 1:7). The guilt offering—making things right? Jesus paid a debt he didn't owe because we owed a debt we couldn't pay. The whole system was pointing somewhere. And it was pointing to him.

Fourth, you can't approach God on your own terms. The offerings had to be done God's way—the right animal, the right method, at the right place. God set the terms, and the worshiper followed them. That's not because God is controlling. It's because he's holy, and he knows what it takes for broken people to come into his presence and survive.

TALKING POINTS

1. **The burnt offering required the worshiper to bring an animal without any defect—the very best they had.** What does it look like to give God your best instead of your leftovers? Where are you tempted to give God the minimum?

2. **The peace offering ended with a shared meal—a celebration in God's presence.** How does the idea of eating a meal with God change the way you think about worship? How does this connect to what Christians do when they take the Lord's Supper?

3. **The guilt offering required not only a sacrifice but also making things right with the person you had wronged—repaying what you took plus twenty percent.** Why do you

think God required both forgiveness and restitution? Is there someone in your life you need to make things right with?

4. **The fire on the altar never went out.** What do you think that constant flame would have meant to an Israelite lying in their tent at night? What reminds you of God's constant presence in your life?

5. **Each of these offerings points forward to something Jesus would do.** Which offering's connection to Jesus stands out to you the most, and why?

The sacrifices were never the final answer. They were repeated day after day, year after year, because they could only cover sin temporarily—they couldn't remove it for good. Leviticus itself hints that something better was coming.

But for the Israelites standing in the wilderness, surrounded by the glow of that never-ending fire, the sacrificial system was an extraordinary gift. It meant they could approach a holy God and live. They could deal with their sin and not be destroyed. They could sit down to eat in the presence of the Almighty.

The protocols weren't there to keep them out. They were there because of who lived inside—and because he wanted them close. And that's still how it works.

Turn the page.

2

THE BEST DAY AND THE WORST DAY

Imagine you've been picked for the starting lineup in the biggest game of the season. Not just picked—chosen by the coach personally, in front of the whole team. You've been training all week. Your gear is laid out. Your family is in the stands. Everything has been building toward this moment.

Game day comes. You play your best. Every pass connects. Every play works. The crowd is on its feet. The final buzzer sounds and your team wins. People are cheering. Your coach is smiling. You did it. Everything you prepared for actually happened, and it was even better than you imagined.

Now imagine that before you've even left the court, before the cheering has died down, one of your teammates does something reckless—something the coach had specifically told everyone not to do—and in an instant, the celebration is over. The best day of your life becomes the worst. Just like that.

That's Leviticus 8–10. These three chapters tell the story of the greatest worship service in Israel's history and the catastrophe that followed it. They contain some of the most triumphant verses in the Old Testament and some of the most devastating. And they happen on the same day.

At the end of Exodus, the tabernacle was built and the glory of God moved in. In the first seven chapters of Leviticus, God gave the instructions for how the sacrifices should work. But there was still a missing piece. The tabernacle was ready. The sacrificial system was designed. But there were no priests to run it.

Think of it this way. The building was constructed. The operating manual was written. But nobody had been hired, trained, or authorized to do the work. Without priests, the entire system sat idle. The sacrifices couldn't be offered. The people couldn't approach God. The tabernacle was a beautiful tent with no one to serve in it. That's where Leviticus 8 begins.

PREPARING THE PRIESTS

God had chosen Aaron—Moses' brother—to be Israel's first high priest, and Aaron's four sons to serve as priests under him. But you didn't just wake up one morning and start the job. The ordination process took seven full days, and every detail mattered.

Moses gathered the entire congregation of Israel to watch. This wasn't a private ceremony. The people needed to see that their priests had been properly appointed by God, not by their own ambition. Everything that followed was done publicly, in front of witnesses.

First, Moses washed Aaron and his sons with water—an outward symbol of the inner cleansing the job required. Then he dressed Aaron in the high priest's garments: the robe, the sash, the breastpiece with twelve stones representing the twelve tribes of Israel, and a gold plate on his forehead engraved with the words "Holy to the LORD." When Aaron put on those clothes, he was putting on the weight of his office. He would carry all of Israel into God's presence every time he served.

Then came the anointing oil. Moses poured it over Aaron's head, consecrating him—setting him apart for sacred work. The tabernacle and all its furniture were anointed too. The oil connected everything: the place, the person, and the purpose. All of it belonged to God.

After the anointing came the sacrifices. Three offerings were made during the ordination: a purification offering to deal with sin, a burnt offering to express total dedication, and a special ordination offering. For this last one, Moses took blood from the ram and put it on the tip of Aaron's right ear, the thumb of his right hand, and the big toe of his right foot.

That's a strange image, right? But the symbolism was powerful. The ear, the hand, the foot—they represented the whole person. Aaron's ears were consecrated to hear God's word. His hands were consecrated to do God's work. His feet were consecrated to walk in God's ways. From head to toe, he belonged to God now.

This process repeated for seven days. Seven days of sacrifices. Seven days of staying inside the tabernacle courtyard without leaving. Seven days of preparation before the priests could begin their actual work.

Why seven? Because seven was the number of completion and creation in Israel's world. God made the world in seven days. Now, in seven days, he was creating something new—a priesthood that would serve as the bridge between a holy God and his sinful people.

THE EIGHTH DAY

Then came the eighth day. And everything changed. The eighth day was the first day of a new beginning. The training was over. The ordination was complete. For the first time in Israel's history, Aaron would step forward as high priest and offer sacrifices on behalf of the people.

Moses told Aaron and the congregation what to expect: "This is what the Lord has commanded you to do, so that the glory of the Lord may appear to you." Did you catch that? God had promised to show up. If Aaron did everything right—if the sacrifices were offered correctly and the priests performed their duties faithfully—the glory of the Lord himself would appear.

The anticipation must have been almost unbearable. Every Israelite in the camp knew what was at stake. They had seen God's glory on Mount Sinai. They had watched it fill the tabernacle. Now it was going to appear again, and this time it would be in response to their worship.

Aaron got to work. He offered a purification offering and a burnt offering for himself first—because even the high priest was a sinner who needed forgiveness before he could represent others. Then he offered sacrifices on behalf of the people: a purification offering, a burnt offering, a grain offering, and a peace offering. Every type of sacrifice except the guilt offering was represented. This wasn't about one specific sin. It was about dedicating the entire nation to the worship of God.

When the sacrifices were complete, Aaron lifted his hands

and blessed the people. Then he and Moses went together into the tent of meeting—into God's dwelling place. When they came out, they blessed the people again.

And then it happened. "The glory of the Lord appeared to all the people. Fire came out from the presence of the Lord and consumed the burnt offering and the fat portions on the altar."

God sent fire from heaven. Not a natural fire, not something sparked by human hands—fire straight from the presence of God, falling on the altar and consuming the sacrifice. It was the ultimate sign of acceptance. God was saying, "I see your worship. I receive it. I am here."

The people's response was immediate and overwhelming. They shouted for joy. Then they fell facedown on the ground. Both reactions made perfect sense. The joy came from knowing that God had accepted them. The falling came from realizing just how close they were to a power beyond anything they could comprehend. If this fire could consume what was on the altar, it could consume them too.

It was the greatest moment in Israel's worship life. Everything had worked. The tabernacle, the sacrifices, the priesthood—it all came together, and God showed up in blazing, unmistakable glory.

And then, two verses later, everything fell apart.

STRANGE FIRE

Nadab and Abihu were Aaron's two oldest sons. They had been through the entire ordination process. They had assisted their father in the sacrifices. They had watched fire fall from heaven. They knew the rules.

And on that same day—the greatest day in Israel's history—they did something God had not commanded.

Each of them took a censer, put fire in it, added incense, and offered it before the Lord. The text calls it "unauthorized fire" or "strange fire." Scholars have debated for centuries exactly what they did wrong. Did they use fire from the wrong source? Did they mix the incense incorrectly? Did they barge into a part of the tabernacle that was off-limits? We don't know the precise infraction. But we know the key phrase: "contrary to his command."

In a system where every detail mattered—where God had spent seven chapters explaining how the sacrifices worked and seven days training the priests to do them correctly—Nadab and Abihu improvised. They decided to approach God on their own terms instead of his.

The result was immediate and devastating. "Fire came out from the presence of the Lord and consumed them, and they died before the Lord."

The same fire. The same divine presence that had just consumed the sacrifice in acceptance now consumed the priests in judgment. Two verses earlier, fire from God was the best thing that had ever happened to Israel. Now it was the worst.

Moses turned to Aaron and said, "This is what the Lord spoke of when he said, 'Among those who approach me I will be proved holy; in the sight of all the people I will be honored.'"

And then three of the most heartbreaking words in the Bible: "Aaron was silent." Not angry. Not arguing. Not asking why. Silent. A father who had just watched two of his sons die, standing in the wreckage of what should have been the best day of his life, with nothing to say.

THE AFTERMATH

What followed was almost as painful as the deaths themselves. Aaron and his surviving sons, Eleazar and Ithamar, were told they could not mourn. No tearing their clothes. No traditional grieving rituals. They had to stay at their post in the tabernacle. The rest of Israel could weep for Nadab and Abihu, but the priests couldn't—because their duty to God came before everything, even their grief.

The bodies were carried out of the camp by Aaron's cousins, still wearing the priestly garments that were supposed to symbolize their holy calling. Those garments became their burial clothes.

God then spoke directly to Aaron—one of the only times in the entire book of Leviticus that God addressed Aaron without going through Moses. He told Aaron that the priests must never drink wine before entering the tabernacle. The placement of this command has led many readers to wonder if alcohol played a role in what Nadab and Abihu did. The text doesn't say so directly, but the warning is clear: the priests needed clear minds. Their job required them to "distinguish between the holy and the common, and between the unclean and the clean." There was no room for carelessness.

The chapter ends with a quieter moment. Moses discovered that Aaron's surviving sons had burned the meat of a purification offering instead of eating it as instructed. He was furious—hadn't they just witnessed what happened when priests disobeyed? But Aaron stepped in. His sons hadn't been careless or rebellious. They were overwhelmed. After everything that had happened that day, they didn't feel worthy to eat the sacred meal. Aaron asked Moses, "Would the Lord have been satisfied if I had eaten it today?"

Moses heard this, and he was satisfied. God, it seems, is more gracious to those who stumble out of reverent fear than to those who barge in out of reckless presumption.

WHAT THIS MEANS FOR US

First, serving God is an honor, and honors come with weight. The priests didn't choose themselves—God chose them. But being chosen meant accepting a standard that was higher, not lower, than what everyone else faced. The closer you are to God, the more seriously he takes your conduct. As Jesus would say centuries later, "From everyone who has been given much, much will be demanded" (Luke 12:48).

Second, God will not be worshiped on our terms. Nadab and Abihu's sin wasn't that they worshiped a false god. They were in the right place, doing a recognizable religious act. But they did it their way instead of God's way, and that was enough. Sincerity without obedience isn't worship. It's presumption.

Third, obedience is not optional. Chapters 8–9 repeat a phrase over and over: "as the Lord commanded." Everything Moses and Aaron did followed God's instructions exactly. That obedience led to fire from heaven in acceptance. Nadab and Abihu's disobedience—doing what God "had not commanded"—led to fire from heaven in judgment. The contrast couldn't be sharper.

Fourth, Jesus is the better priest. Aaron needed purification offerings for his own sin before he could serve. His sons failed catastrophically on their very first day. The whole system depended on flawed humans who could get it wrong at any moment. The New Testament book of Hebrews makes the case that Jesus is the high priest who never failed, never sinned, never offered unauthorized fire. He didn't need to offer a sacrifice for himself. He offered himself as the sacrifice—once, perfectly, and for all time.

TALKING POINTS

1. **The ordination process took seven days.** Why do you think God required such lengthy, detailed preparation before the priests could begin serving? What does this tell us about how God views worship and service?

2. **When fire fell from heaven and consumed the sacrifice, the people shouted for joy and then fell facedown.** Why both reactions? Have you ever experienced something that was both wonderful and overwhelming at the same time?

3. **Nadab and Abihu's sin was doing something God "had not commanded."** Why is it dangerous to assume we can approach God however we want? How might this apply to the way we worship today?

4. **Aaron was told he couldn't mourn his sons publicly.** That sounds incredibly harsh. Why do you think God required this? What does it tell us about the cost of serving in God's presence?

5. **At the end of the chapter, Moses accepted Aaron's explanation for why his sons didn't eat the offering.** What does this moment tell us about the difference between careless disobedience and reverent fear?

The eighth day of the priesthood began with the greatest worship service Israel had ever seen and ended with two dead priests and a grieving father who couldn't shed a tear. It was the best day and the worst day, all in one.

But notice what didn't happen. God didn't leave. The tabernacle still stood. The fire on the altar still burned. Aaron, despite his grief, was still high priest. The system wasn't scrapped. God corrected, judged, warned—and then kept going. His plan to dwell among his people was bigger than even this disaster.

The priesthood would continue. But everyone who witnessed that day would never forget the lesson: the God who draws near in grace is the same God who demands to be treated as holy. Both things are true. Both things matter. And the people who serve him most closely are the ones who must never forget it.

Turn the page.

3

WHAT MAKES SOMETHING UNCLEAN?

In the movie *Monsters, Inc.*, the entire monster world runs on a single belief: human children are toxic. One touch from a kid and a monster is contaminated. When a single child's sock makes it through the door and lands on a monster's back, the response is instant—alarms blare, hazmat teams arrive in full gear, the sock is neutralized, and the contaminated monster is shaved, scrubbed, and decontaminated. The whole factory shuts down. Everyone panics. All because of a sock.

It seems ridiculous—until you realize the monsters aren't wrong to take contamination seriously. They just have the wrong information about what's actually dangerous.

Now imagine a community that had the *right* information about what was dangerous. Imagine God himself telling a nation, "Here's what contamination looks like. Here's what makes you unclean. Here's what will keep you out of my presence if you don't deal with it." That community would take those rules very seriously—because the contamination wasn't imaginary. The God living in their camp was real, his holiness was real, and the consequences of bringing something impure into his presence were very, very real.

That's exactly what Leviticus 11–15 is about. These five chapters are the Bible's most detailed instructions on cleanness and uncleanness—and while they might seem strange to us today, they mattered enormously to the people who lived with God's presence in their backyard.

Before we jump in, we need to understand something crucial: "unclean" doesn't mean "sinful." That's the biggest mistake people make when reading these chapters. They assume that when Leviticus says something is "unclean," it means "morally wrong." But that's not what the word means here. Unclean meant something more like "not in the right condition to enter God's presence." It was a status, not a sin. You didn't confess your way out of it. You waited, you washed, and sometimes you brought a sacrifice—not for forgiveness, but for restoration.

Almost everyone became unclean at some point. Having a baby made you unclean. Getting sick made you unclean. Touching a dead animal made you unclean. These were normal parts of life—not evil actions. But they were all conditions that had to be addressed before a person could come back to the tabernacle and worship.

Think of it this way. There's nothing wrong with playing in the mud, but you don't walk into the White House caked in dirt. You clean up first—not because playing outside was bad, but because where you're going demands a certain condition. Leviticus is teaching Israel that living with a holy God in their camp required constant attention to their condition. Holiness touched everything—what they ate, what they touched, and what happened to their bodies.

YOU ARE WHAT YOU EAT

The food laws are probably the most famous—and most debated—part of this section. God told Israel exactly which animals they could eat and which ones they couldn't.

For land animals, the rule was straightforward: an animal had to both chew its cud and have split hoofs. Cows, sheep, and goats qualified. Pigs didn't, because even though they have split hoofs, they don't chew their cud. Camels didn't qualify either—they chew their cud but don't have the right kind of hoofs. Both qualifications were required. No exceptions.

For sea creatures, the test was fins and scales. Fish that swim normally in the water were clean. Anything else—shellfish, eels, crabs—was off the menu.

For birds, no general rule was given, but a long list of forbidden species was provided. Almost all of them were birds of prey or scavengers—eagles, vultures, hawks, owls—birds that eat other animals or feed on dead things.

Insects were mostly off-limits, with one exception: locusts and grasshoppers with jointed legs for hopping were permitted. Everything else that crawled or swarmed was unclean.

Why these rules? People have debated this for centuries. Some say it was about health—pork can carry disease, shellfish can spoil quickly. There's probably some truth to that, but hygiene doesn't explain everything. Some clean animals are just as risky as some unclean ones, and if the rules were purely about health, it's hard to explain why Jesus later declared all foods clean.

The most compelling explanation goes deeper. The clean animals were the ones that fully conformed to the patterns of their world. Fish that swim with fins and scales are doing what fish are supposed to do. Land animals with split hoofs and cud-chewing are behaving like the standard domesticated animals of Israel's world. Birds of prey violate a fundamental rule of God's creation—they consume blood and flesh, which was forbidden for everyone. Creatures that "swarm" move in chaotic, unpredictable ways that don't fit neatly into any category.

In other words, the clean animals were pictures of wholeness and order. The unclean animals blurred boundaries and broke patterns. And here's the deeper point: God was teaching Israel to see holiness everywhere, even in what they ate. Just as God had chosen Israel from among all the nations and set them apart, the food laws set apart certain animals from others. Every single meal was a reminder: "You are my people. You are different. You are set apart."

This is why the New Testament's treatment of the food laws is so important. When Jesus declared all foods clean, and when Peter had a vision of unclean animals on a sheet and heard God say, "Do not call anything impure that God has made clean," the message was stunning. The wall between Jew and Gentile was coming down. God's holiness was no longer marked by dietary rules but by the transformation of the heart. The food laws had done their job—they had taught Israel about holiness for over a thousand years. Now something greater had come.

CHILDBIRTH AND UNCLEANNESS

This is one of the most misunderstood chapters in the Bible.

After giving birth, a woman was considered unclean for a period of time—seven days for a boy (followed by thirty-three more days of purification), and fourteen days for a girl (followed by sixty-six more days). During this time she couldn't enter the tabernacle or touch anything sacred.

Let's be very clear about what this does *not* mean. It does not mean childbirth was sinful. It does not mean the baby was unclean. It does not mean women were considered less valuable. God himself had commanded people to "be fruitful and multiply." Having children was a blessing, not a curse.

So why the uncleanness ruling? The issue was the physical reality of childbirth—specifically the discharge of blood that followed delivery. In Leviticus, any flow of blood outside of sacrifice was a problem. Blood represented life, and losing blood pointed toward weakness and death. The only blood that belonged in the tabernacle was sacrificial blood, deliberately offered in the way God had prescribed. Any other blood— whether from childbirth, injury, or illness—was incompatible with the place where the God of life dwelled.

The purification period wasn't a punishment. It was a recognition that the physical process of bringing new life into the world, as beautiful and God-given as it was, left the mother in a condition that needed time and cleansing before she could reenter God's holy space.

When the purification period ended, the mother brought a burnt offering and a purification offering. The priest made atonement for her—not because she had done anything wrong, but to ritually restore her to full access to the tabernacle. Then she was clean again.

This is exactly what Mary, the mother of Jesus, did after his birth. Luke 2:22–24 describes Mary and Joseph bringing the offerings prescribed in Leviticus 12. Even the mother of the Son of God followed these instructions. That tells you everything you need to know: this law wasn't about sin. It was about the physical realities of life in a fallen world and the holiness of the God who lived among his people.

SKIN DISEASES

Leviticus 13–14 deal with what older Bible translations call "leprosy," but the word covers a much broader range of conditions—rashes, sores, infections, swellings, discolorations, and chronic skin problems of all kinds. It even includes mold and mildew that appeared on clothing or on the walls of houses.

The process was detailed. If someone noticed an unusual mark on their skin, they went to the priest—not because the priest was a doctor, but because the priest was the one responsible for determining whether someone was ritually clean or unclean. The priest would examine the spot, looking for specific signs: Was it deeper than the surrounding skin? Had the hair in the area turned white? Was it spreading?

If the signs were inconclusive, the person was quarantined for seven days and then examined again. If the condition had spread, the person was declared unclean. If it hadn't, they were declared clean. Some cases required a second quarantine of another seven days.

A person declared unclean had to live outside the camp. They wore torn clothes, let their hair hang loose, covered the lower part of their face, and called out "Unclean! Unclean!"

whenever someone approached. It sounds brutal—and it was a hard way to live. But the purpose wasn't cruelty. It was protection. A person with an active, spreading skin condition was a living picture of decay, of the body breaking down. That condition was incompatible with the holiness of God's dwelling place, and it could potentially spread to others.

But here's the part people often miss: the system wasn't just about keeping people out. It was about bringing them back in.

Leviticus 14 describes an elaborate restoration ceremony for someone whose skin disease had healed. The priest went outside the camp to meet the person—God's representative went to them, not the other way around. Two birds were brought. One was killed over fresh water, and the other was dipped in the blood and water, then released alive into the open field. The healed person was sprinkled with the blood-water mixture, washed, shaved, and waited seven more days. On the eighth day—the day of new beginnings—they brought offerings to the Lord, and the priest applied blood to their right ear, right thumb, and right big toe. Sound familiar? It's the same ritual used for the ordination of the priests. The healed person was being restored, given a fresh start, welcomed back into the community and back into God's presence.

The message was clear: uncleanness didn't have to be permanent. There was always a way back.

BODILY DISCHARGES

The final chapter in this section deals with the most personal topic of all: bodily discharges. The chapter is structured in a careful balance—two sections about men, two about women—

making it clear that this wasn't a problem unique to one gender. Everyone was affected.

For men, the chapter addresses both chronic conditions (ongoing discharges that signaled illness) and normal biological functions. For women, it addresses both regular menstruation and abnormal, prolonged bleeding. In every case, the discharge made a person temporarily unclean. Anything they sat on or lay on became unclean too. Anyone who touched them or the things they had touched also became unclean.

The more serious conditions—chronic infections and prolonged bleeding—required waiting seven days after the condition ended, washing, and bringing two birds as offerings. The less serious conditions required simply bathing and waiting until evening.

None of these conditions were sins. No confession was required. No word of forgiveness was spoken. The point was simpler and more profound: the physical realities of the human body—the messy, leaking, sometimes failing body—were incompatible with the perfect holiness of God's presence.

The chapter ends with a verse that ties the whole section together: "You must keep the Israelites separate from things that make them unclean, so they will not die in their uncleanness for defiling my tabernacle, which is among them."

There it is. The reason behind five chapters of rules about food, childbirth, skin disease, and bodily functions. God was living in the camp. His tabernacle was right there, surrounded by tents full of ordinary people who ate, bled, got sick, gave birth, and sometimes broke out in rashes. The purity laws were the system that made it possible for a perfectly holy God and deeply imperfect people to share the same space without someone getting destroyed.

WHAT THIS MEANS FOR US

First, holiness touches everything. Leviticus doesn't allow for a divided life—sacred on Sunday, ordinary the rest of the week. What you eat, what you touch, what happens to your body—it all matters to God. The New Testament carries this forward: "Whether you eat or drink or whatever you do, do it all for the glory of God (1 Corinthians 10:31).

Second, uncleanness is a picture of what sin does. While being "unclean" wasn't the same as sinning, the purity system taught Israel to feel the effects of living in a broken world. Disease, decay, and death were constant reminders that something had gone wrong in creation. Every time an Israelite had to separate from the community and wait to be restored, they experienced in miniature what sin does on a cosmic scale—it separates us from God.

Third, God always provides a way back. Every unclean condition had a remedy. Every excluded person had a path to restoration. The priest went outside the camp to meet the healed person. The sacrifices were offered. The person was welcomed back. God never wanted people to stay separated. He wanted them close—and he built the entire system to make that possible.

Fourth, Jesus fulfilled these laws in person. He touched lepers and made them clean instead of becoming unclean himself. He was touched by a woman with a twelve-year discharge of blood, and power went out from him, not impurity into him. He declared all foods clean. He broke every barrier that separated people from God—not by ignoring holiness, but by being so holy that uncleanness couldn't survive his touch.

TALKING POINTS

1. **The food laws reminded Israel at every meal that they were set apart by God.** What are some ways Christians today can be reminded of their identity in everyday activities?

2. **Being "unclean" wasn't the same as being sinful—it was a condition, not a moral failure.** Why is it important to understand the difference? How might confusing the two lead to harmful thinking?

3. **The priest went outside the camp to meet the person healed of a skin disease.** What does that tell you about God's heart for people who feel excluded? How does this connect to how Jesus treated outcasts?

4. **Leviticus 15:31 says the purity laws existed to protect the people from "defiling my tabernacle, which is among them."** How does knowing that God physically lived in their camp change the way you understand these rules?

5. **Jesus touched people who were unclean and made them clean instead of becoming unclean himself.** What does this tell you about who Jesus is and what his power can do?

Five chapters of regulations about food, childbirth, rashes, and bodily functions. Not exactly the material that makes it into Sunday school songs. But underneath all the strange details, these chapters are asking one of the most important questions in the Bible: How can imperfect, messy, sometimes falling-apart human beings live in the presence of a perfect God?

Leviticus 11–15 answered that question with a system of boundaries, waiting periods, washings, and sacrifices. It worked—but it was exhausting. There was always another condition to manage, another uncleanness to address, another sacrifice to bring. The system kept God close, but it never solved the underlying problem. People kept getting sick. Bodies kept breaking down. Uncleanness kept coming back.

What Israel needed wasn't a better purity system. They needed someone whose holiness was so powerful that it didn't just avoid contamination—it reversed it. Someone who could touch the unclean and make them whole.

They were still waiting for him. But he was coming.

Turn the page.

4

THE DAY OF ATONEMENT

In almost every great adventure story, there's a moment when one person has to go alone into the most dangerous place.

In *The Lord of the Rings*, Frodo has to carry the ring into the heart of Mount Doom. In *Harry Potter and the Deathly Hallows*, Harry walks alone into the Forbidden Forest to face Voldemort. In *The Hunger Games*, Katniss volunteers as tribute and steps forward while everyone else watches in silence. The crowd can't follow. The friends can't help. One person goes in, and everyone else holds their breath—because everything depends on what happens next.

Leviticus 16 is that moment for Israel. Once a year, on the most sacred day in the entire calendar, the high priest did something no one else was allowed to do. He passed through the curtain that separated the Holy Place from the Most Holy Place—the inner room of the tabernacle where God's presence dwelled above the ark of the covenant. He went in alone. No other priest could accompany him. No one from the congregation could be inside the tent of meeting at all. The entire nation waited outside while one man walked into the presence of the living God.

If he did everything right, Israel's sins would be forgiven, the tabernacle would be cleansed, and the people would get a fresh start. If he didn't—well, they already knew what happened when someone approached God the wrong way. Nadab and Abihu had found out.

This was the Day of Atonement. And it was the most important day of the year.

WHY THIS DAY EXISTED

The chapter opens with a grim reminder: "The LORD spoke to Moses after the death of the two sons of Aaron who died when they approached the LORD." That's not a random detail. It's the reason these instructions were given. Nadab and Abihu had entered God's presence carelessly, on their own terms, and they died. The Day of Atonement was God's answer to the question their deaths raised: How can anyone safely enter the Most Holy Place?

But the Day of Atonement wasn't just about protecting the high priest. It was about a much bigger problem.

Remember everything we learned in the last chapter about cleanness and uncleanness? All those rules about food, skin diseases, bodily discharges, and contamination? Here's what was happening behind the scenes. Every time an Israelite sinned or became unclean, it was like a stain spreading toward the tabernacle. Sin didn't just affect the sinner—it polluted the place where God lived. Day after day, week after week, the uncleanness of the people accumulated on the tabernacle and its furniture like grime building up on a window.

The regular sacrifices described in Leviticus 1–7 dealt with individual sins as they happened. But they couldn't handle all of it. Some sins went unconfessed. Some uncleanness went unnoticed. Over the course of a year, the contamination built up. If it was never dealt with comprehensively, God's holiness and Israel's sinfulness would eventually become incompatible. God would have to leave. His presence would depart from the tabernacle, and Israel would be on their own.

The Day of Atonement was God's solution—a once-a-year, top-to-bottom, total cleansing of everything. It was the day when every sin, every defilement, and every trace of contamination was removed so that God could keep living among his people.

Think of it as a deep clean. The regular sacrifices were like daily tidying—picking up messes as they happened. The Day of Atonement was like pulling out every piece of furniture, scrubbing the floors and walls, and making the whole house spotless again. Without it, the mess would eventually become unlivable.

DRESSED LIKE A SERVANT

The first thing Aaron had to do was change his clothes. Normally the high priest dressed like royalty. His regular garments were stunning—a blue robe, a breastpiece embedded with twelve precious stones, gold thread, an embroidered sash, and a golden plate on his forehead that read "Holy to the LORD." When Aaron walked through the camp in his priestly vestments, everyone knew he was the most important religious figure in the nation.

But on the Day of Atonement, he took all of that off. Instead, he put on a simple white linen tunic, linen undergarments, a linen sash, and a linen turban. Plain. Unadorned. The kind of clothes a servant might wear.

Why? Because on this day, the high priest wasn't walking among his fellow Israelites. He was walking into the throne room of the King of kings. Among people, his position was the highest in the land. Before God, he was nothing but a servant. The simple linen said what needed to be said: no human being enters God's presence on the strength of their own importance. You come humbly, or you don't come at all.

Before putting on the linen, Aaron bathed his entire body in water. Clean clothes on a clean body. Everything about his preparation said the same thing: what you're about to do is dangerous, sacred, and unlike anything else you do all year.

BEHIND THE CURTAIN

The ceremony had multiple stages, but the heart of it was what happened behind the curtain. Aaron first sacrificed a bull as a purification offering for himself and his family. Even the high priest was a sinner. He couldn't cleanse the nation until he'd been cleansed himself.

Then he took a censer full of burning coals from the altar, filled his hands with finely ground incense, and carried it behind the curtain into the Most Holy Place. There, he put the incense on the coals so that a cloud of fragrant smoke filled the room, covering the mercy seat—the golden lid on top of the ark of the covenant where God's presence appeared. The smoke served as a screen between Aaron and the raw, overwhelming presence of God. Without it, he would die.

Then came the blood. Aaron went back out, collected the blood of the bull he had sacrificed, returned behind the curtain, and sprinkled it on the mercy seat and seven times in front of it. This blood purified the Most Holy Place from the contamination of the priests' sins.

Next, he sacrificed one of two goats—the one selected by lot "for the Lord"—as a purification offering for the people. He carried that blood behind the curtain too, and sprinkled it on the mercy seat just as he had done with the bull's blood. This cleansed the Most Holy Place from the contamination of the people's sins.

After the inner room was clean, Aaron moved outward. He purified the Holy Place—the outer room of the tabernacle where the incense altar, lampstand, and bread table stood. Then he went into the courtyard and purified the great altar of burnt offering, sprinkling it with the blood of both the bull and the goat. From the inside out, every inch of the tabernacle was being scrubbed clean.

The whole time this was happening, no one else was allowed inside the tent of meeting. Aaron was completely alone with God. The congregation waited outside, watching the entrance of the tabernacle, hoping to see their high priest walk back out alive.

THE GOAT THAT CARRIED IT ALL AWAY

Then came the most vivid moment of the entire ceremony. Two goats had been brought to the tabernacle at the beginning of the day. Lots were cast over them—one "for the Lord," one to be sent away. The first goat had already been sacrificed. Now the second goat was brought forward, alive.

Aaron placed both hands on the goat's head—not one hand, as in the regular offerings, but both. And then he did something that happened at no other time in the entire year. He confessed. Out loud, in front of everyone, the high priest spoke over the goat all the wickedness, rebellion, and sin of the entire nation. Every lie. Every act of cruelty. Every moment of unfaithfulness. Every sin that had been committed in secret and never addressed. All of it—spoken aloud and placed on the head of this animal.

Then a man who had been appointed for the task led the goat out of the camp, away from the tabernacle, away from the people, deep into the wilderness. The goat carried Israel's sins into a remote, desolate place—and it never came back.

The symbolism was impossible to miss. This was a living picture of what God was doing with their sin. He wasn't just forgiving it in some invisible, abstract way. He was removing it. Taking it away. Sending it so far from his people that it could never find its way back.

The blood of the first goat purified the tabernacle. The second goat removed the sin from the people. Together, they accomplished complete atonement—a total, comprehensive dealing with everything that stood between Israel and God.

WHAT THE PEOPLE DID

The Day of Atonement wasn't just a spectacle the people watched. They had responsibilities too.

God commanded the entire nation to "deny yourselves"—a

phrase that included fasting, self-examination, and prayer. No one could work. It was a complete sabbath rest. The idea was that while the high priest was doing his work inside the tabernacle, the people outside were doing their own work—the inner work of repentance, humility, and honest reckoning with their sin.

The ritual alone wasn't enough. If someone fasted on the outside but felt no grief over their sin on the inside, the Day of Atonement meant nothing to them. The prophet Isaiah would later confront Israel on exactly this point: people who fasted on the Day of Atonement while still exploiting their workers and ignoring injustice (Isaiah 58). God wasn't interested in empty rituals. He wanted hearts that matched the ceremony.

When everything was finished—the blood sprinkled, the goat sent away, the sacrifices completed—the text says something beautiful: "Before the LORD, you will be clean from all your sins."

Clean. Not partially clean. Not mostly forgiven. Completely clean. Every sin dealt with. Every stain removed. Every barrier between God and his people cleared away for another year. The nation could exhale. They could start over.

WHAT THIS MEANS FOR US

First, sin accumulates, and it has to be dealt with completely. The Day of Atonement teaches that you can't just handle sin one piece at a time and hope for the best. Eventually, a comprehensive reckoning is needed. The good news is that God himself provided that reckoning. He didn't leave Israel to figure it out on their own. He designed the solution and gave it to them.

Second, someone had to go in on our behalf. No ordinary Israelite could enter the Most Holy Place. Only the high priest, properly prepared, properly clothed, carrying the right blood, on the right day, could go behind the curtain and survive. The people needed a representative—someone to stand before God for them because they couldn't stand there themselves.

Third, the Day of Atonement points directly to Jesus— and he fulfilled both goats. The New Testament book of Hebrews builds its entire argument around this chapter. Jesus is the high priest who entered not an earthly tabernacle but heaven itself. He didn't bring the blood of bulls and goats—he brought his own blood. He didn't need to offer a sacrifice for his own sins first because he had none. And he didn't have to do it year after year, because his sacrifice was so complete, so perfect, so final that it never needs to be repeated.

And like the scapegoat, Jesus carried our sins away. Isaiah 53 says, "The LORD has laid on him the iniquity of us all." John the Baptist introduced Jesus with words that echo this chapter: "Look, the Lamb of God, who takes away the sin of the world." Jesus didn't just cover sin. He removed it—carried it into a place so remote it can never come back.

When Jesus died, the massive curtain in the temple—the one that separated the Holy Place from the Most Holy Place, the same curtain that had kept everyone out for over a thousand years—tore in two, from top to bottom. God ripped it open. The way in was no longer restricted to one man, on one day, once a year. It was open to everyone, forever.

Fourth, the Day of Atonement was an annual event. It had to be repeated every year because the blood of animals could never permanently solve the problem of sin. It pointed to something better. It was a shadow of the real thing. And when the real thing came—when Jesus offered himself once for all—the shadow was no longer needed.

TALKING POINTS

1. **The high priest changed from his magnificent robes into plain white linen before entering God's presence.** What does this teach us about how we should approach God? What "royal clothes" might we need to take off?

2. **Aaron had to offer a sacrifice for his own sin before he could represent the people.** Why is it significant that Jesus didn't need to do this? What does that tell you about who he is?

3. **The scapegoat carried Israel's sins into the wilderness and never came back.** What does it feel like to know that God doesn't just forgive sin but removes it completely? How does this change the way you think about your own failures?

4. **The people were commanded to "deny yourselves" on the Day of Atonement—to fast, pray, and examine their hearts.** Why wasn't it enough for the high priest to do the ritual on their behalf? What role does personal repentance play in receiving God's forgiveness?

5. **When Jesus died, the temple curtain tore from top to bottom.** What do you think that moment meant for the people who saw it? What does it mean for us today?

Once a year, for as long as the tabernacle and then the temple stood, the Day of Atonement played out the same way. The high priest dressed in white. The bull was killed. The blood was carried behind the curtain. The goat was sent into the wilderness. The people fasted, prayed, and waited. And at the end of the day, the word rang out: *Clean.*

But every year they had to do it again. The blood of animals could cleanse, but it couldn't cure. It could cover, but it couldn't transform. The Day of Atonement was a masterpiece of divine mercy—but it was always pointing beyond itself, to a day when one final high priest would walk through one final curtain, carrying not the blood of goats but his own, and finish the job once and for all.

That day came. And the curtain never closed again.

Turn the page.

5

WHY BLOOD IS DIFFERENT

In the *Harry Potter* series, some of the most powerful magic in the entire wizarding world isn't cast with a wand. It runs through veins.

When Lily Potter sacrificed herself to save her infant son, her blood created a protection so strong that Voldemort—the most dangerous dark wizard alive—couldn't touch Harry without burning. Years later, when Dumbledore sent Harry to live with his mother's sister, he explained why: the blood connection kept the protection alive. And when Voldemort finally managed to use Harry's blood in a dark ritual to rebuild his body, even that act backfired because the blood carried something Voldemort hadn't counted on. Lily's sacrifice lived in it.

In the wizarding world, blood isn't just a liquid. It carries identity, power, and protection. It connects people. It saves lives.

J. K. Rowling didn't invent that idea. She borrowed it from a tradition that goes back thousands of years—all the way to Leviticus 17. Because long before anyone imagined Hogwarts, God told Israel something extraordinary about blood:

it carries life itself, and he has reserved it for one purpose that matters more than anything else.

THE HINGE OF THE BOOK

Leviticus 17 is a short chapter—only sixteen verses—but it punches way above its weight. Scholars sometimes call it the "hinge" of the entire book, because it connects everything that came before with everything that comes after.

The first sixteen chapters of Leviticus were focused on worship—the sacrifices, the priesthood, clean and unclean, the Day of Atonement. Starting in chapter 18, the book shifts to focus on how Israel should live—their relationships, their ethics, their daily behavior. Chapter 17 sits right in the middle, linking both halves with one powerful theme: blood is sacred, and it belongs to God.

This chapter lays down four rules, and every one of them comes back to the same point. Together, they form one of the most important theological statements in the entire Old Testament. So let's take them one at a time.

RULE #1: BRING EVERY SACRIFICE TO THE TABERNACLE

The first law is blunt. If any Israelite slaughtered an ox, a lamb, or a goat—whether inside the camp or outside it—and did not bring it to the entrance of the tent of meeting as an offering to the Lord, that person was "guilty of bloodshed." They would be "cut off from their people."

That's an extreme punishment for what might seem like a minor infraction. Why would it matter where you killed an animal? Because this wasn't really about geography. It was about loyalty.

The problem God was addressing shows up in verse 7: "They must no longer offer any of their sacrifices to the goat idols to whom they prostitute themselves." Even while God was physically dwelling in the middle of their camp—even after the glory of the Lord had appeared, after fire had fallen from heaven, after the Day of Atonement had been established—some Israelites were still sneaking off to sacrifice to other gods. The "goat idols" were demonic beings that people in the ancient world believed haunted the wilderness, often pictured in goat-like form, similar to the satyrs of Greek mythology. Some Israelites were hedging their bets, offering sacrifices to these creatures on the side, just in case.

God's response was absolute. Every sacrifice had to come to the tabernacle. Every animal slaughtered for a religious purpose had to be brought to the priest, offered at the altar, with the blood splashed properly and the fat burned as an offering. No exceptions. No side deals. No secret altars out in the fields.

The word God used to describe this divided loyalty was "prostitution." That's not casual language. It's the language of a broken relationship. God wasn't just Israel's ruler or their benefactor. He was their covenant partner—the one who had rescued them from Egypt, given them his law, and moved into their camp. Sacrificing to other gods wasn't just a mistake. It was betrayal.

The requirement to centralize all sacrifice at the tabernacle also protected the sacrificial system itself. If people could offer animals anywhere they wanted, there was no oversight, no accountability, and no guarantee that the blood would be handled properly. The tabernacle was the one place where everything was done according to God's instructions, under the supervision of his priests. Keeping sacrifice centralized kept it holy.

RULE #2: DO NOT EAT BLOOD

The second rule is the most famous verse in the chapter—and one of the most important in the entire book. "I will set my face against any Israelite or any foreigner residing among them who eats blood, and I will cut them off from the people."

Then comes the reason: "For the life of a creature is in the blood, and I have given it to you to make atonement for yourselves on the altar; it is the blood that makes atonement for one's life." There are two enormous ideas packed into this single verse.

First, blood equals life. This wasn't just a religious belief—it was observable reality. When an animal lost its blood, it died. Blood was what kept the body alive. So when God said "the life of a creature is in the blood," he was saying that blood represented the most precious thing in the physical world: life itself. To consume blood was to treat life casually. It was to take something sacred and make it ordinary.

This principle went all the way back to Noah. After the flood, when God gave humanity permission to eat meat for the first time, he gave one restriction: "You must not eat meat that has its lifeblood still in it" (Genesis 9:4). Even then, centuries before Leviticus, God was teaching humanity that blood—and the life it represented—belonged to him.

Second, God assigned blood for atonement. This is the part that changes everything. God didn't just say blood was special. He said he had *given* it to Israel for a specific, sacred purpose: to make atonement on the altar. The blood of the animal served as a ransom. When an Israelite sinned—when they did something that deserved death—an animal's blood was offered in their place. The animal's life was given so the person's life could be spared.

That's why eating blood was such a serious offense. It wasn't just disrespectful. It was taking something God had designated for the holiest purpose imaginable—the saving of human lives—and using it for a common meal. Imagine someone taking a life-saving medicine and pouring it down the drain because they liked the color. That's the kind of offense God is describing. Blood was the currency of atonement. Wasting it, consuming it, or treating it like regular food was an insult to the God who had provided it as the only means of restoring the relationship between himself and his sinful people.

Notice, too, who this law applied to: not just Israelites, but also "any foreigner residing among them." The sanctity of blood wasn't a rule for one ethnic group. It reflected a universal truth about life, death, and the God who owned both.

RULE #3: HUNTERS MUST DRAIN THE BLOOD

The third rule extended the principle to everyday life. If an Israelite went hunting and killed a wild animal or bird that was clean to eat, they had to drain its blood and cover it with earth. They couldn't just cook the animal as-is. The blood had to be removed and returned to the ground—given back to the earth, which is where God had formed life in the first place.

This rule meant that even something as ordinary as hunting for dinner became a moment of theological awareness. Every time an Israelite killed an animal for food, the act of draining the blood and covering it was a reminder: *This life belonged to God. I'm not the ultimate owner here. The life in this animal was a gift, and the blood that carried it is not mine to consume.*

It's easy to skip over a rule like this, but think about what it would have done to the daily rhythm of Israelite life. You couldn't eat a meal without being reminded that life is sacred, that blood is reserved for God, and that every act of taking life—even for food—carries weight. There was no such thing as a thoughtless meal in Israel. Every dinner pointed back to the altar and forward to the truth that life and death are in God's hands alone.

RULE #4: DON'T EAT ANIMALS FOUND DEAD

The final rule dealt with animals that weren't slaughtered at all—animals that died on their own or were killed by predators. If an Israelite came across one of these and ate from it, they became unclean. They had to wash their clothes, bathe in water, and remain unclean until evening.

The penalty here was lighter than the others—no mention of being "cut off"—because the situation was different. The person hadn't deliberately consumed blood in defiance of God. But the animal's blood hadn't been properly drained either, so eating it still created a problem. The uncleanness had to be addressed.

This rule closed the last loophole. Whether you were offering a sacrifice at the tabernacle, hunting in the wilderness, or stumbling across a dead animal on the road, the principle was the same: blood matters, and it has to be handled with care.

WHY THIS CHAPTER MATTERS SO MUCH

Leviticus 17 might seem like a chapter about ancient dietary rules. But it's actually laying the theological foundation for the most important event in human history.

When the chapter says "the life of a creature is in the blood" and "the blood makes atonement for one's life," it's establishing a principle that runs like a thread through the entire Bible—from Genesis to Revelation. Blood carries life. Life can be exchanged. An innocent life, offered in the right way, can ransom a guilty one. This is the logic of every sacrifice Israel ever offered, and it's the logic that would eventually explain the cross.

The author of Hebrews put it plainly: "Without the shedding of blood there is no forgiveness" (Hebrews 9:22). That statement is essentially a summary of Leviticus 17:11. The entire sacrificial system—and everything it pointed to—rests on the truth that blood is life, and life is what atonement costs.

WHAT THIS MEANS FOR US

First, God does not share his worship. The command to bring every sacrifice to the tabernacle—and to stop offering to goat idols—was a demand for exclusive loyalty. God wasn't one option among many. He was the only God, the only source of atonement, the only one who could save. The same is true in the New Testament. There is one mediator between God and humanity, one sacrifice that actually works, one name under heaven by which we must be saved.

Second, life is sacred because it belongs to God. The blood rules weren't arbitrary dietary restrictions. They were training Israel to see every living creature as belonging to its Creator. You can't treat life carelessly when you've been taught that the blood sustaining it belongs to someone else. This principle extends far beyond food—it shapes how we view every human being, every act of violence, and every question about the value of life.

Third, atonement costs something real. Blood isn't a symbol. It's the substance of life. When God said he had given blood for atonement, he was saying that forgiveness isn't free—it requires the giving of a life. In the Old Testament, it was the life of animals. In the New Testament, it was the life of God's own Son. The cost never went down. It went up—infinitely.

Fourth, Jesus turned the prohibition on its head. In the Old Testament, consuming blood was the gravest offense because blood was reserved for the altar. But when Jesus said, "Whoever eats my flesh and drinks my blood has eternal life" (John 6:54), he was making a staggering claim. The blood that was always too sacred to consume was now being offered directly to his people—because his blood accomplished what animal blood never could. It didn't just cover sin temporarily. It removed it permanently. The thing that had always been off-limits was now the very thing being given. Leviticus said, "Don't drink the blood—it's for atonement." Jesus said, "Drink my blood—because I *am* the atonement."

TALKING POINTS

1. **God described Israel's worship of goat idols as**

"prostitution." Why would he use such a strong word? What does this tell you about how God views divided loyalty?

2. **Leviticus 17:11 says God "gave" blood to Israel for atonement.** What does it mean that blood was a gift from God, not something the people came up with on their own? How does this change the way you think about sacrifice?

3. **Even hunting for dinner required an Israelite to drain the blood and cover it with earth.** What effect do you think this daily practice had on how they thought about life and food? Are there ways Christians should be more thoughtful about everyday activities?

4. **The author of Hebrews says, "Without the shedding of blood there is no forgiveness."** Why do you think God designed the system this way? Why couldn't forgiveness work without blood?

5. **In the Old Testament, blood could never be consumed.** In the New Testament, Jesus tells his followers to "drink his blood." How can both instructions be right? What changed between Leviticus and the Last Supper?

Sixteen verses. Four rules. One theme: blood is life, and life belongs to God. It's a chapter that most people skip when they read Leviticus—if they read Leviticus at all. But buried in these regulations about where to slaughter animals and what to do with their blood is the theological engine that powers the entire story of the Bible. Sin requires atonement. Atonement requires blood. Blood carries life. And only God has the authority to decide how that life is given and received.

For over a thousand years, Israel lived inside this system.

They brought their animals to the tabernacle and the temple. They watched the blood splash against the altar. They drained their game and covered the blood with earth. And every time they did, they were being reminded of a truth they couldn't yet fully see: that one day, the blood of something far greater than a bull or a goat would be poured out—not on an altar of bronze, but on a cross of wood. And when it was, the need for every other sacrifice would finally, permanently, be finished.

Turn the page.

6

BE HOLY BECAUSE I AM HOLY

Here's a question that sounds simple but isn't: What does it actually look like to be a good person? Not just in big, dramatic moments—not just "would you save someone from a burning building?" Of course you would. Everyone says yes to that. The harder question is what goodness looks like on a random Tuesday. How do you treat people when no one's watching? What do you do with your money? How do you talk about the kid at school nobody likes? Do you cheat when you know you won't get caught?

In the movie *Wonder*, Auggie Pullman's teacher, Mr. Browne, gives his class a precept on the first day of school: "When given the choice between being right or being kind, choose kind." It's a simple idea, but the rest of the movie shows how incredibly difficult it is to actually live it out—day after day, choice after choice, especially when being kind costs you something.

Leviticus 18–20 is God's version of that challenge. After sixteen chapters about sacrifices, priests, purity, and the Day of Atonement, the book takes a dramatic turn. God stops talking about what happens at the altar and starts talking about what happens everywhere else—in homes, in fields, in marketplaces, in courtrooms, and in the most private corners of people's lives. And the whole section is built on one sentence that might be the most important command in the entire Old Testament: "Be holy because I, the LORD your God, am holy."

THE FRAME: DON'T LIVE LIKE EVERYONE ELSE

Chapters 18 and 20 form a frame around the central chapter 19. They deal with the same basic subject—the practices of the nations around Israel that God's people must avoid—and together they explain both the *what* (chapter 18) and the *consequences* (chapter 20).

God opens chapter 18 with a blunt command: "You must not do as they do in Egypt, where you used to live, and you must not do as they do in the land of Canaan, where I am bringing you." Israel had spent four hundred years in Egypt. They were about to move into Canaan. Both cultures were soaked in practices that God called detestable—things that violated the boundaries he had built into creation.

The chapter then lists those practices. Most of them involve sexual boundaries—who you can and cannot have an intimate relationship with. The list is long and specific, and it covers situations that were disturbingly common in the ancient world: relationships between family members, adultery, and other violations of the boundaries God established for marriage and intimacy when he created human beings as male and female.

Mixed into this list is one of the most horrifying practices of the ancient world: child sacrifice. The Canaanites worshiped a god called Molech, and part of that worship involved offering children in fire. It's hard for us to imagine, but this was a real religious practice in the nations surrounding Israel. God's prohibition was absolute: "Do not give any of your children to be sacrificed to Molech, for you must not profane the name of your God."

The chapter ends with a warning that makes the stakes unmistakable. The reason Israel was getting the land of Canaan in the first place was that the Canaanites had become so corrupt that "the land itself vomited them out." God was expelling them because of these very practices. And if Israel adopted the same behaviors, the same thing would happen to them. The land would reject them too.

Chapter 20 returns to these same practices but adds something chapter 18 didn't include: specific penalties. The punishments were severe—often death—because in God's eyes these weren't minor mistakes. They were attacks on the very order of creation, on the sanctity of the family, and on the holiness that was supposed to define his people.

The severity can be hard for us to understand. But the point wasn't cruelty. It was clarity. God was saying, "I am deadly serious about these boundaries." In a world where every surrounding nation had normalized practices that destroyed families, exploited the vulnerable, and degraded human dignity, Israel was supposed to be visibly, unmistakably different. The penalties matched the stakes.

THE HEART: WHAT HOLINESS ACTUALLY LOOKS LIKE

If chapters 18 and 20 are the frame, chapter 19 is the masterpiece hanging inside it. Many scholars believe this chapter is the center of the entire book of Leviticus—and maybe even the center of the entire first five books of the Bible.

It opens with the command that defines everything: "Be holy because I, the LORD your God, am holy." But then, instead of leaving "holiness" as an abstract idea floating in the clouds, God does something remarkable. He fills it in with specifics. He takes holiness out of the tabernacle and plants it in the middle of everyday life. And the picture that emerges is breathtaking.

Holiness looks like taking care of your parents. "Each of you must respect your mother and father" (19:3). This isn't a suggestion. It's the foundation of a stable society, and God puts it near the top of the list.

Holiness looks like feeding the hungry. "When you reap the harvest of your land, do not reap to the very edges of your field or gather the gleanings of your harvest. Leave them for the poor and the foreigner" (19:9–10). Israelite farmers were legally required to leave food behind for people who had nothing. Caring for the poor wasn't optional charity—it was built into the economic system by God's own command.

Holiness looks like honesty. "Do not steal. Do not lie. Do not deceive one another" (19:11). Simple, direct, and comprehensive. No cheating, no fraud, no half-truths.

Holiness looks like paying people fairly. "Do not hold back the wages of a hired worker overnight" (19:13). If someone worked for you, you paid them that day. You didn't make them wait while you used their money for yourself. God noticed how employers treated workers.

Holiness looks like protecting the vulnerable. "Do not

curse the deaf or put a stumbling block in front of the blind" (19:14). This goes far beyond the literal meaning. It's a principle: don't exploit people's weaknesses. Don't take advantage of someone who can't see what you're doing or can't hear what you're saying about them.

Holiness looks like justice. "Do not pervert justice; do not show partiality to the poor or favoritism to the great, but judge your neighbor fairly" (19:15). Notice that this cuts both ways. You can't rig the system for the rich, but you also can't bend the rules just because someone is poor. Justice means treating everyone the same, regardless of status.

Holiness looks like refusing to gossip. "Do not go about spreading slander among your people" (19:16). In a world without social media, gossip was the most powerful tool for destroying someone's reputation. God treated it as a matter of holiness.

Holiness looks like honest confrontation instead of hidden resentment. "Do not hate a fellow Israelite in your heart. Rebuke your neighbor frankly so you will not share in their guilt" (19:17). If someone wrongs you, don't simmer in silent bitterness. Talk to them. Deal with it directly. Hatred that hides is more dangerous than conflict that surfaces.

Holiness looks like using honest measurements. "Do not use dishonest standards when measuring length, weight, or quantity. Use honest scales and honest weights" (19:35–36). Even the way you weigh someone's flour at the market is a holiness issue. God cared about the accuracy of your scales.

Holiness looks like loving the immigrant. "When a foreigner resides among you in your land, do not mistreat them.

The foreigner residing among you must be treated as your native-born. Love them as yourself, for you were foreigners in Egypt" (19:33–34). This is extraordinary. God commanded Israel to love the outsider as much as they loved their own people—and he grounded it in their own experience. "You know what it feels like to be the stranger. Don't do that to someone else."

And then, right in the middle of all these practical instructions, comes the verse that Jesus would later call the second greatest commandment in the entire Bible: **"Love your neighbor as yourself. I am the LORD"** (19:18).

This isn't a New Testament invention. It comes straight from Leviticus 19. When Jesus was asked to name the greatest commandment, he answered with Deuteronomy 6:5—love God with all your heart—and then added this verse from Leviticus as the second. The apostle Paul said this single command summarizes the entire law (Galatians 5:14). James called it "the royal law" (James 2:8). It's the most quoted Old Testament verse in the entire New Testament. And it was sitting here all along, in the book most people skip.

THE REFRAIN: "I AM THE LORD"

One of the most striking features of chapter 19 is a phrase that repeats over and over, sixteen times in a single chapter: "I am the LORD." After the command to respect your parents: "I am the LORD." After the command to leave food for the poor: "I am the LORD your God." After the command not to steal or lie: "I am the LORD." After the command to love the foreigner: "I am the LORD your God, who brought you out of Egypt."

Why does God keep saying this? Because every single law in this chapter rests on one foundation: God's own identity. The reason you don't steal isn't just that stealing is wrong. The reason you don't steal is that the God who rescued you from slavery is a God of honesty, and you are his people. The reason you leave grain for the poor isn't just compassion. It's because the God who provided manna in the wilderness is a God who feeds the hungry, and you are supposed to act like him.

"Be holy because I am holy" doesn't mean "follow a bunch of rules." It means "become like me." Every law in this chapter is a portrait of God's own character—his justice, his generosity, his honesty, his care for the vulnerable, his hatred of exploitation—translated into instructions that ordinary people could practice in their ordinary lives.

WHAT THIS MEANS FOR US

First, *holiness* is not just a church word. It belongs in kitchens, classrooms, workplaces, and playgrounds. Leviticus 19 makes it impossible to separate your relationship with God from the way you treat the people around you. You can't worship God at the altar on Saturday and cheat your neighbor on Monday. As one scholar put it, God's holiness was to be on display "from the corners of your beard to the corners of your fields."

Second, these laws were grounded in grace, not earning. God didn't say, "Keep these rules and I'll make you my people." He said, "I am the LORD your God, who brought you out of Egypt"—and *then* gave the commands. The obedience came after the rescue, not before it. Israel didn't keep the law to earn God's love. They kept it because they already had it.

Third, loving your neighbor is the heart of the law. Jesus didn't pull this idea out of thin air. He pulled it out of Leviticus. And the context of Leviticus 19 makes clear that "neighbor" isn't limited to people who look like you, live near you, or share your background. By verse 34, the command has expanded to include the foreigner—the person who is most unlike you. Love that only extends to people who are easy to love isn't the kind of love God is describing.

Fourth, God cares about the details. Honest scales. Fair wages. Leftover grain for the poor. Not gossiping. Not holding grudges. These aren't minor matters to God. If holiness is about becoming like him, then it shows up in the smallest choices—how you speak, how you spend your money, and how you treat the person no one else notices.

TALKING POINTS

1. **Leviticus 19 shows that holiness touches every part of life—food, work, relationships, money, and speech.** Which of the laws in this chapter surprised you the most? Which one do you think would be hardest for people to follow today?

2. **God commanded Israel to leave the edges of their fields unharvested so the poor could eat.** What would a modern version of this law look like? How can communities today build care for the poor into their everyday systems?

3. **"Love your neighbor as yourself" comes from Leviticus, not the New Testament.** Why do you think Jesus chose this verse as the second greatest commandment? What does it mean to love someone "as yourself"?

4. God told Israel to love foreigners because "you were foreigners in Egypt." How does your own experience of being an outsider—at a new school, in a new neighborhood, on a new team—shape the way you should treat others who are outsiders?

5. The phrase "I am the LORD" appears sixteen times in Leviticus 19. Why do you think God kept repeating it? What does it add to the commands it follows?

Three chapters. One frame and one masterpiece. The frame—chapters 18 and 20—draws a line between God's people and the practices of the surrounding nations. It says, "This is what you are *not*." The boundaries are firm, the stakes are high, and the consequences are real.

But the masterpiece—chapter 19—paints the picture of what God's people *are*. They are people who feed the hungry, pay workers on time, refuse to gossip, tell the truth, welcome the stranger, protect the vulnerable, and love their neighbors as themselves. Not because they're trying to earn God's approval, but because the God who rescued them is that kind of God, and they are learning to look like him.

"Be holy because I am holy."

It wasn't a command to be perfect. It was an invitation to become like the one who made them, loved them, and refused to let them settle for anything less than his best.

Turn the page.

7

A CALENDAR BUILT ON A STORY

Think about the holidays you celebrate every year. Christmas, Thanksgiving, the Fourth of July, maybe your birthday. Now think about what they actually do. They don't just give you a day off school. They tell a story. Thanksgiving reminds you of people who survived a dangerous journey and gave thanks. The Fourth of July commemorates the moment a nation declared its independence. Christmas celebrates a birth that changed the world.

Now imagine that your entire calendar—every holiday, every special meal, every day off—was designed by God himself. Not just to give you a break, but to walk you through the most important events in your nation's history, year after year, so you would never forget who you were, who saved you, and where you were going.

That's what Leviticus 21–24 sets up. These four chapters cover the qualifications for priests, the standards for sacrificial animals, the complete calendar of Israel's sacred festivals, and a few final laws that tie the section together. If the previous chapters told Israel *how* to be holy, these chapters tell them *when*—giving them a rhythm of worship that would shape their identity for centuries and point forward to the coming of Jesus in ways they couldn't yet imagine.

HIGHER STANDARDS FOR THE PRIESTS

Before getting to the festivals, Leviticus 21–22 addresses the people who would lead Israel's worship: the priests.

We've already seen that holiness in Israel worked in layers. Every Israelite was called to be holy. But the priests were called to an even higher standard because they worked closest to God's presence. And the high priest, who entered the Most Holy Place once a year, had the highest standard of all.

These chapters spell out what that higher standard looked like. Ordinary priests could become ritually unclean by attending the funeral of a close family member—a parent, child, or sibling—but they couldn't defile themselves for anyone outside that circle. The high priest couldn't attend any funeral at all, not even for his own mother or father. He could never leave the sanctuary during his period of service, and he could only marry a woman who had never been married before.

Priests with certain physical defects—blindness, lameness, disfigurement—were not allowed to serve at the altar, though they could still eat the priestly food and participate in other ways. This sounds harsh to modern ears, and it's important to understand what was going on. The restriction wasn't a statement about the worth of people with disabilities. It was a symbolic requirement: since the priests represented God's perfection before the people, and since the sacrificial animals had to be physically flawless, the priests who offered them had to match that standard of wholeness. Everything in the tabernacle system pointed toward the perfection of God, and every element—animal, priest, and ritual—had to reflect it.

This is actually one of the places where the New Testament brings enormous relief. The book of Hebrews makes clear that Jesus is the ultimate high priest—one who is "holy, blameless, pure, set apart from sinners, exalted above the heavens" (Hebrews 7:26). Because he fulfilled the priestly role perfectly, the old physical requirements are no longer needed. Now every Christian is part of a "royal priesthood," and the qualification for service is spiritual, not physical.

Chapter 22 turns to the sacrificial animals themselves and makes the same point from the other side. The animals brought to the altar had to be without blemish—no blindness, no broken limbs, no sores, no deformity. You couldn't bring God your leftovers and call it worship. The offering had to cost something, and it had to represent the best you had.

The message across both chapters is consistent: what comes into God's presence must reflect the holiness of the God who lives there. The priests. The animals. The worship. All of it pointed to a perfection that no human could fully achieve on their own—which is exactly why a better priest and a better sacrifice were always needed.

THE SACRED CALENDAR

Chapter 23 is one of the most important chapters in the entire book. It lays out Israel's complete festival calendar—seven appointed times that structured the entire year around the story of God's relationship with his people.

The Sabbath (23:1–3). The calendar begins with the weekly rhythm: six days of work, one day of complete rest. The Sabbath wasn't just a day off. It was the sign of Israel's covenant with God, going all the way back to creation. When God finished making the world, he rested—not because he was tired, but because everything was complete and good. The Sabbath invited Israel to step into that same rest every week, to stop striving and trust that the God who made everything was still holding it together.

Then came the annual festivals, arranged in two clusters—three in the spring and three in the fall, with one in between.

Passover and the Festival of Unleavened Bread (23:4–8). The year began in the spring with a one-two punch. On the fourteenth day of the first month, Israel celebrated Passover—the night God's angel passed over the homes marked with lamb's blood and rescued his people from slavery in Egypt. The very next day began the seven-day Festival of Unleavened Bread, during which no yeast was allowed. The bread without yeast symbolized leaving behind the old life of bondage and starting fresh.

For the New Testament reader, the connections are impossible to miss. Jesus was crucified during Passover. He is "our Passover lamb," as Paul wrote (1 Corinthians 5:7)—the one whose blood marks God's people and delivers them from death.

The Festival of Firstfruits (23:9–14). During the week of Unleavened Bread, on the day after the Sabbath, the Israelites brought the first sheaf of their barley harvest and waved it before the Lord. It was an act of faith and gratitude—offering the very first sign of the harvest before knowing whether the rest would come in.

Paul picked up this image and applied it directly to Jesus. "Christ has indeed been raised from the dead, the firstfruits of those who have fallen asleep" (1 Corinthians 15:20). Just as the first sheaf guaranteed a full harvest to come, Christ's resurrection guarantees the future resurrection of everyone who belongs to him. And the timing fits perfectly: Jesus rose from the dead on the first day of the week, during the Passover season—the exact day the firstfruits were offered.

The Festival of Weeks (23:15–22). Fifty days after Firstfruits came the Festival of Weeks—later called Pentecost, from the Greek word for "fifty." This celebrated the completion of the wheat harvest. The Israelites brought two loaves of bread baked with leaven and presented them to God alongside prescribed sacrifices. The harvest that began with a single sheaf had now produced finished bread.

In the New Testament, the Holy Spirit came upon the early church on the day of Pentecost. The connection is stunning: Christ's resurrection (the firstfruits) produced the church (the bread). Just as the wheat harvest turned raw grain into loaves, the risen Jesus gathered his followers into a community empowered by his Spirit. And just as the Festival of Weeks eventually came to commemorate the giving of the Law at Sinai, the Holy Spirit at Pentecost wrote God's law on the hearts of Christians—exactly as the prophet Jeremiah had promised in the new covenant (Jeremiah 31:33).

Even the detail about leaven matters. Unlike the unleavened bread of Passover, these loaves were baked with yeast. The church, unlike Christ, is not sinless. It is made up of imperfect people—yet God still receives it as an offering.

And tucked into this festival passage is a familiar command: "When you reap the harvest of your land, do not reap to the very edges of your field or gather the gleanings. Leave them for the poor and the foreigner." Even in celebration, Israel was never allowed to forget the vulnerable.

The Festival of Trumpets (23:23–25). After a gap of several months, the fall festivals began on the first day of the seventh month with the blowing of trumpets. This was a sacred assembly—a day of rest and worship that called the people together and prepared them for the most solemn season of the year. The trumpet was understood as the voice of God summoning his people into his presence.

In the New Testament, the trumpet becomes associated with the return of Christ: "The Lord himself will come down from heaven, with a loud command, with the voice of the archangel and with the trumpet call of God" (1 Thessalonians 4:16). The Festival of Trumpets foreshadowed the ultimate gathering of God's people at the end of the age.

The Day of Atonement (23:26–32). We've already covered this in detail in Chapter 4, but it appears again here as part of the calendar. On the tenth day of the seventh month, the entire nation fasted, rested completely, and waited while the high priest entered the Most Holy Place to cleanse the tabernacle and remove the people's sins. It was the most solemn day of the year.

The Festival of Tabernacles (23:33–43). Five days after Atonement came the most joyful festival of all. For seven days, the Israelites lived in temporary shelters made of branches—a reenactment of their wilderness journey after leaving Egypt. They had spent forty years living in tents, dependent on God for food, water, and direction every single day. The Festival of Tabernacles made them relive that dependence and then celebrate the fact that God had brought them through.

By Jesus' time, the festival had taken on rich additional traditions. Water was ceremonially poured on the altar as a prayer for rain and a symbol of spiritual blessing. A great candelabrum was lit in the temple courts. It was during this very festival that Jesus stood up and declared, "Let anyone who is thirsty come to me and drink," and also, "I am the light of the world." He was claiming that everything the festival pointed to was fulfilled in him.

THE LAMPSTAND, THE BREAD, AND ONE DRAMATIC INCIDENT

Chapter 24 shifts to two ongoing elements of tabernacle worship before closing with a striking narrative.

The Israelites were commanded to provide pure olive oil to keep the lampstand burning continually in the Holy Place, and to bake twelve loaves of bread—one for each tribe—to be set on the golden table before the Lord every Sabbath. The lamp provided light; the bread symbolized God's provision and his covenant relationship with all twelve tribes. Together, they painted a picture: someone was home. The lights were on, food was on the table, and God was present with his people.

Jesus later drew on both images. He called himself "the light of the world" and "the bread of life." At the Last Supper, he took bread, broke it, and said, "This is my body." The bread of the presence became the bread of communion—God's ongoing provision for his people in a new and deeper way.

The chapter ends with a jarring story. A man with an Israelite mother and an Egyptian father got into a fight and blasphemed God's name. The community didn't know what to do, so they brought him to Moses, who consulted God. The verdict was severe: the blasphemer was taken outside the camp and stoned.

Attached to this ruling came a set of broader laws about justice, including the famous "eye for eye, tooth for tooth" principle. Despite its reputation, this law was actually designed to limit vengeance, not encourage it. If someone knocked out your tooth, you couldn't kill their whole family in retaliation. The punishment had to match the crime—no more, no less. And the same law applied to Israelites and foreigners alike: "You are to have the same law for the foreigner and the native-born."

WHAT THIS MEANS FOR US

First, worship isn't improvised—it's designed by God. The festivals, the Sabbath, the priestly standards, the quality of the offerings—none of this was left to human preference. God decided how, when, and by whom he would be worshiped. This doesn't mean worship has to be rigid or joyless. The Festival of Tabernacles was a week-long party. But it means worship begins with what God wants, not what we feel like doing.

Second, the calendar tells the gospel. Passover, Unleavened Bread, Firstfruits, Pentecost, Trumpets, Atonement, Tabernacles—they trace the arc of salvation from rescue to resurrection to the gift of the Spirit to the final gathering. The entire Christian story was embedded in Israel's calendar centuries before Jesus was born.

Third, Jesus fulfilled every festival. He is the Passover Lamb. He is the Firstfruits from the dead. His Spirit came at Pentecost. He is the final atonement. He is the living water and the light of the world proclaimed at Tabernacles. The festivals were shadows; he is the reality they pointed to.

Fourth, rest is not laziness—it's trust. The Sabbath principle running through this chapter says that stopping your work and trusting God is itself an act of worship. In a world that never stops producing, consuming, and performing, the invitation to rest is more radical than it sounds.

TALKING POINTS

1. **The Festival of Firstfruits required offering the very first grain before the rest of the harvest came in.** What does it look like to give God the "first" of something rather than the leftovers? Why does the order matter?

2. **Jesus made his boldest claims—"I am the living water" and "I am the light of the world"—during the Festival of Tabernacles.** Why do you think he chose that specific festival to reveal these truths?

3. **The priests were held to a higher standard than ordinary Israelites.** Do you think it's fair that leaders are judged more strictly? Why or why not?

4. **The Sabbath was about trusting God enough to stop working.** What makes rest difficult for you? What would it look like to practice real, trusting rest in your life?

5. **The "eye for eye" law was meant to limit revenge, not encourage it.** How does knowing this change the way you read that verse? What does it tell you about God's view of justice?

Seven appointed times. One story. From Passover to Tabernacles, from the first sheaf of barley to the final day of celebration in shelters made of branches, Israel's entire year was structured around one truth: God had rescued them, God was with them, and God was leading them somewhere.

The priests who led the worship had to be set apart. The animals they offered had to be the best. The calendar they followed had to be observed exactly as God designed it. None of this was arbitrary. Every detail—every loaf on the table, every lamp burning in the Holy Place, every trumpet blast in the fall—was part of a single, unified story that started with a lamb's blood on a doorpost in Egypt and would end with a lamb's blood on a cross outside Jerusalem.

They didn't know the ending yet. But every year, when they walked through the calendar God had given them, they were rehearsing it.

Turn the page.

8

THE GREAT RESET

If you've ever played Monopoly, you know how the game ends. One player owns Boardwalk, Park Place, and half the board loaded with hotels. Everyone else is slowly going bankrupt, handing over rent they can't afford every time they land on the wrong property. The game drags on, but the outcome is already decided. The rich player keeps getting richer. Everyone else keeps getting crushed. It's fun for the winner. It's miserable for everyone else.

Now imagine a rule that said every so often, all the properties go back to their original owners. All debts are erased. All the money gets redistributed. The board resets, and everyone starts fresh. The player with all the hotels can't stay on top forever. The player who's been mortgaging everything just to survive doesn't stay at the bottom forever. Nobody's permanent fortune—and nobody's permanent failure—is allowed to stand.

You'd never put that rule in a board game. But God put it in real life. Leviticus 25–27 describes one of the most radical ideas in the history of the world. God looked at the nation he was building—a world of farms and fields, debts and labor, wealth and poverty—and he designed a reset button. Every seven years, the land rested. Every fifty years, everything went back to the way it started. Debts were canceled. Slaves were freed. Families got their land back. The rich couldn't stay rich forever by exploiting the poor, and the poor weren't trapped in poverty for life. It was called the Year of Jubilee. And it might be the most radical economic idea in the history of the world.

REST FOR THE LAND

Before getting to the Jubilee, God established a smaller cycle: the Sabbath Year. Just as people rested every seventh day, the land rested every seventh year. For six years, the Israelites could plant, prune, and harvest. But in the seventh year, they couldn't sow their fields, prune their vineyards, or organize a formal harvest. Whatever grew on its own was available to everyone: owners, workers, poor people, even animals. But no one could farm it commercially.

This was an enormous act of trust. Imagine being a farmer and God telling you to stop farming for an entire year. "What will we eat?" was the obvious question, and God answered it directly: "I will send you such a blessing in the sixth year that the land will yield enough for three years." The Sabbath Year forced Israel to rely on God rather than on their own effort.

But it did something else too. It reminded them of a truth that ran through the entire book of Leviticus: the land didn't belong to them. It belonged to God. They were stewards, not owners. Letting the land rest every seven years was a physical way of acknowledging that everything they had—their fields, their food, their livelihood—was a gift from someone else.

FREEDOM FOR EVERYONE

After seven cycles of Sabbath Years (seven times seven, forty-nine years) came the fiftieth year: the Jubilee. On the Day of Atonement in that year, trumpets sounded throughout the land. And the announcement they carried was unlike anything the ancient world had ever heard: "Proclaim liberty throughout the land to all its inhabitants." (That sentence, by the way, is inscribed on the Liberty Bell in Philadelphia. The founders of the United States borrowed it directly from Leviticus 25:10.)

The Jubilee had three main features, and each one was revolutionary.

First, all land returned to its original family. When Israel entered the promised land, God divided it among the twelve tribes and their families. Each family received a portion—their inheritance. Over time, though, life happened. Droughts. Bad harvests. Debts. Some families had to sell their land to survive. Without the Jubilee, wealthy families would have accumulated more and more property while poor families lost everything permanently. The Jubilee prevented that. No matter how much land you'd lost, in the fiftieth year it all came back. Your family's inheritance was restored.

This also meant that land was never really "sold" in Israel. When you bought a field, you were actually buying the right to farm it until the next Jubilee. The price was based on how many harvests were left before the land reverted. God stated the principle plainly: "The land must not be sold permanently, because the land is mine and you reside in my land as foreigners and strangers." No Israelite was ever the ultimate owner of anything. God was.

Second, all Israelite servants were set free. When people fell into serious debt, they sometimes had to work for someone else to pay it off—a kind of indentured servitude. But the Jubilee put a limit on it. No matter how much you owed, when the fiftieth year arrived, you went free. You returned to your family and your ancestral land, and you started over.

Even before the Jubilee, God regulated how servants were treated. An Israelite who worked for another Israelite couldn't be treated like a slave. They had to be treated like a hired worker. The reason God gave was stunning: "Because the Israelites are my servants, whom I brought out of Egypt, they must not be sold as slaves." God had freed them from bondage in Egypt. He wasn't about to let them be permanently enslaved to each other.

Third, the Jubilee created an economy of generosity and trust. God knew that some people would worry about the practical details. If you couldn't permanently own land or permanently hold servants, how would the economy function? His answer was woven into the laws themselves. Relatives could buy back property for family members who'd fallen on hard times. Interest-free loans were required for fellow Israelites in poverty. And the entire system was underpinned by the promise that God himself would provide.

The Jubilee was God's way of saying that no economic system should allow permanent winners and permanent losers. Poverty should never be a life sentence. Wealth should never become an empire. Every generation deserved a fresh start.

THE JUBILEE AND JESUS

Here's where Leviticus 25 becomes one of the most important

chapters in the entire Bible for understanding what Jesus came to do. There's almost no evidence that Israel ever actually practiced the Jubilee. The idea was magnificent, but the nation apparently never carried it out. The rich didn't want to give back land. The powerful didn't want to free their workers. The Jubilee remained an unfulfilled promise—a vision of justice and freedom that Israel kept failing to live up to.

So the prophets picked up the language and pointed it forward. Isaiah wrote in Isaiah 61 about a coming servant who would "proclaim good news to the poor," "freedom for the captives," "release from darkness," and "the year of the Lord's favor"—all Jubilee language, aimed at a future day when the reset would finally happen.

And then, in Luke 4, Jesus walked into the synagogue in his hometown of Nazareth, was handed the scroll of Isaiah, unrolled it to that exact passage, read it aloud, sat down, and said seven words that changed everything: "Today this scripture is fulfilled in your hearing."

Jesus was announcing that the Jubilee had finally arrived—not as an economic policy but as a person. He was the one who would set captives free. He was the one who would release the oppressed. He was the one who would proclaim the year of the Lord's favor. And the freedom he offered wasn't just freedom from debt or servitude. It was freedom from sin, death, and everything that held people in bondage.

The connection goes even deeper. The Jubilee was proclaimed on the Day of Atonement. You couldn't have freedom without first having forgiveness. The trumpet that announced the Jubilee only sounded after the blood had been sprinkled and the scapegoat had carried the people's sins into the wilderness. Atonement came first; liberty followed.

The same is true with Jesus. His Jubilee, the great reset he came to bring, was only possible because of his death on the cross. Forgiveness of sins made freedom possible. The Day of Atonement made the Year of Jubilee possible. And the early church lived this out, sharing possessions, caring for the poor, and treating every person as an equal inheritor of God's grace.

THE TWO PATHS

After the Jubilee legislation, God laid out two possible futures for Israel. If they obeyed his commands—if they followed the Sabbath Years, practiced the Jubilee, kept the covenant—he promised extraordinary blessings: rain in the right season, abundant harvests, peace in the land, victory over enemies, and above all, his presence. "I will put my dwelling place among you, and I will not abhor you. I will walk among you and be your God, and you will be my people." That final promise was the ultimate blessing. Not just crops and safety. God himself, living among them.

But if they rejected his laws and broke the covenant, the consequences would come in five escalating waves, each one more severe than the last, and each one designed not to destroy but to wake them up. First, disease and defeat. Second, drought and failed crops. Third, wild animals and danger. Fourth, war, siege, and famine. Fifth, and worst of all, exile. God would scatter them among the nations, and the land would finally get the Sabbath rest they had refused to give it.

The curses are hard to read. But two things stand out.

First, God described each stage of punishment as discipline, not revenge. The goal was always repentance. Second—and this is crucial—the chapter doesn't end with exile. It ends with a promise. "But if they will confess their sins and the sins of their ancestors—their unfaithfulness and their hostility toward me... then I will remember my covenant."

Even after the worst-case scenario, God left the door open. Confession and humility could still lead to restoration. The covenant couldn't be permanently broken, because it didn't ultimately depend on Israel's faithfulness. It depended on God's. "I will not reject them or abhor them so as to destroy them completely, breaking my covenant with them. I am the Lord their God."

This pattern (rebellion, punishment, repentance, restoration) would play out over and over in Israel's history. And it points directly to the gospel: God's faithfulness outlasts human failure. His covenant endures even when his people don't.

VOWS AND DEDICATIONS

The book ends with a chapter about vows. These were voluntary promises people made to dedicate themselves, their family members, their animals, their houses, or their land to God. The chapter provides detailed instructions about how to calculate the value of what was promised and how to buy it back if needed.

It might seem like an odd way to end the book. But it actually makes perfect sense. After a chapter full of warnings about what happens when people break their commitments to God, Leviticus closes by addressing commitments that go *beyond* what's required: the extra, voluntary promises that people make when they're moved by gratitude, desperation, or devotion.

The chapter also serves as a bookend for the entire book. Leviticus opened with voluntary offerings in chapters 1–3. It closes with voluntary dedications in chapter 27. The message is the same at both ends: your relationship with God isn't just about obligation. It's about the overflow of a grateful heart.

The final verse wraps it all up: "These are the commands the Lord gave Moses at Mount Sinai for the Israelites." Everything in the book—every sacrifice, every law, every festival, every warning—came from God, delivered through Moses, given at the mountain where God met his people face to face.

WHAT THIS MEANS FOR US

First, God cares about economic justice. The Sabbath Year and Jubilee weren't optional add-ons. They were covenant obligations. God didn't just care about what happened in the tabernacle. He cared about who owned the land, who was trapped in debt, and whether the poor had any hope of getting back on their feet. A community that worships God but ignores economic injustice has missed the point.

Second, everything belongs to God. The land was his. The people were his servants. The wealth, the crops, the animals—all of it was on loan. When we truly believe this, it changes how we hold everything we have. We become stewards instead of owners, and generosity becomes the natural response.

Third, God's discipline is not the same as God's rejection. The escalating curses of Leviticus 26 are frightening, but they're framed as a father disciplining his children, not an enemy destroying his opponents. Even at the very bottom, after exile and scattering, God says, "I will remember my covenant." His faithfulness outlasts our failures.

Fourth, Jesus is the ultimate Jubilee. Every debt canceled. Every captive freed. Every inheritance restored. What Israel never managed to practice, Jesus accomplished in full. When he stood up in that synagogue and said, "Today this scripture is fulfilled," he wasn't exaggerating. He was announcing that the great reset had finally arrived—and it was available to everyone.

TALKING POINTS

1. **The Jubilee guaranteed that no family would be permanently poor and no family would be permanently wealthy.** Do you think this is a good system? What would it look like if something like this existed today?

2. **God told Israel, "The land is mine."** How does the idea that everything ultimately belongs to God change the way you think about your own possessions?

3. **The blessings of Leviticus 26 climax with God's promise to "walk among you and be your God."** Why is God's presence described as the greatest blessing—greater than rain, harvests, or peace?

4. **Even after describing the worst possible punishments, God says, "I will not reject them."** What does this tell you about God's character? How does it compare to the way people usually treat those who've broken their trust?

5. **Jesus announced the Jubilee in Luke 4 but didn't immediately fix every injustice.** Why not? What does it mean that the Jubilee is "already but not yet"?

And so the book ends where it began: at the foot of Mount Sinai, with the voice of God still echoing. Leviticus opened with God calling to Moses from the tent of meeting, giving instructions for how a sinful people could approach a holy God. It closes with the promise that if those people will trust him—with their land, their time, their wealth, their obedience, and their hearts—he will walk among them, dwell with them, and never abandon them.

Between those two bookends stands an entire system designed to answer one question: How can God live with people who aren't like him? The answer involves blood and fire, priests and festivals, clean and unclean, and above all, a relentless, stubborn grace that refuses to give up, even when the people it loves keep getting it wrong.

Leviticus isn't the book people skip because it doesn't matter. It's the book people skip because they don't yet realize how much it does.

www.ingramcontent.com/pod-product-compliance
Lightning Source LLC
Chambersburg PA
CBHW061429050726
47593CB00006B/2279